"I Have Autism"
A Child's First Look at Autism

by Pat Crissey
illustrated by Noah Crissey

This book is dedicated to
my husband, Rob, for his constant
support in all that I do and to my
son Noah, who has always been
willing to lend his artistic talents to
help clarify ideas for the children
with whom I've worked.

Pat Crissey

Post Office Box 24997, Greenville, South Carolina 29616 USA

Call Toll Free 1-800-277-8737 • Fax Toll Free 1-800-978-7379
Online! www.superduperinc.com
E-Mail: custserv@superduperinc.com

Super Duper Publications®

My name is Alex
and I have autism.

I'm not the only kid who has autism. There are other kids who have autism too.

I didn't do anything to get autism.
I was just born with it.

3

You can't tell that I have autism
by looking at me, but my brain works a
little differently sometimes and that
can make some things hard for me.

Sometimes I just don't understand what people are saying to me or what they are feeling.

5

And it's hard for me to figure out what I should say to people. I can't seem to find the right words to say what I want to say. That's because I have autism.

When I don't understand what people say or what's happening, I can say, "I don't understand."

When I don't know what to say,
I try to remember that it's OK to
take my time and think about what I
want to say.

Some things are hard for me to learn, like tying my shoes and answering questions about what I read. I feel dumb when I can't do these things.

But I'm not dumb! There are things I know a lot about and things I do really well. I know all about video games and I remember some things that everyone else forgets.

And when things are hard for me,
I can ask for help.

There are people who want to help me, like my parents, my teachers and other kids.

Sometimes I can't stop thinking about certain things, like video games and dinosaurs.

All I want to do is talk and think about these things. That's because I have autism.

But I can use my reminders to help me stay on-task.

My reminders tell me I can talk about dinosaurs later, but now it is time to work.

Another thing about autism is that some things can bother me a lot! Sometimes I feel all twisted and jumpy when I hear a lot of noise or when we do things differently at school. The other kids don't seem to care that things are noisy or confusing, but I do. That's because I have autism.

When I feel all jumpy I can go
take a break and breathe lots of
air really slow.

18

I have autism, but mainly I'm a
kid and I like to have fun.

I have fun playing video games
with my friend.

Lots of people tell me that I'm a great kid, and I know that they are right. I am a great kid!

I'm a kid who has autism and that's OK.